"A person of power lives in [his or her] sacred self.
I found that the only power that is real in this world is
spiritual ... True power comes from being in harmony
with the forces of the universe."

— Dr. Susan Gregg

Be a Person of Power

Come to know the happiness in every moment when you live from your sacred self! Your sacred self is the essence of who and what you are; it is the part of you that fully understands how sacred and precious *every* experience is.

The exercises in this workbook were designed especially to help you grasp the happiness, personal freedom and power that come from possessing inner peace. Each chapter explores a different aspect of the "way of the Nagual" and provides specific exercises to help you internalize these shamanic teachings. Through these exercises you will learn that *happiness is a state of mind that you have the power to create whenever you want to.*

Finding the Sacred Self is the perfect way to apply the insights of Dr. Gregg's first book, *Dance of Power*—or use it alone as your workbook of personal transformation. Learn meditations to explore alternate realities, "turn up the volume" on your senses, find power spots for yourself wherever you go, banish negative energies from your life and much more.

Change the way you interact with your world and love everything about your life, starting *today*—when you practice the wisdom of the shamans and reclaim your powerful, intuitive, sacred self.

D0190969

ABOUT THE AUTHOR

Dr. Susan Gregg was born and raised in New York City. She graduated in 1972 from the University of Vermont with a BA in Mathematics. At that time she began to explore metaphysics, including transcendental meditation.

After moving to California in the 1980s, Susan met a Mexican Nagual or Shaman, and became his apprentice. When she finished her apprenticeship, the Nagual told her to go out and teach in her own manner.

In 1989 Susan received her Doctorate in Clinical Hypnotherapy. She became a Reverend in the Universal Church of the Master in Santa Clara, California. Susan now lives in Hawaii with her springer spaniel. She is in private practice assisting people in transforming their lives. She lives happily by the beach in a sleepy town, enjoying life on a daily basis.

TO WRITE TO THE AUTHOR

If you wish to contact the author or would like more information about this book, please write to the author in care of Llewellyn Worldwide, and we will forward your request. Both the author and publisher appreciate hearing from you and learning of your enjoyment of this book and how it has helped you. Llewellyn Worldwide cannot guarantee that every letter written to the author can be answered, but all will be forwarded. Please write to:

Dr. Susan Gregg
% Llewellyn Worldwide
P.O. Box 64383-K334, St. Paul, MN 55164-0383, U.S.A.
Please enclose a self-addressed, stamped envelope for reply, or $1.00 to cover costs. If outside the U.S.A., enclose an international postal reply coupon.

FREE CATALOG FROM LLEWELLYN

For more than 90 years Llewellyn has brought its readers knowledge in the fields of metaphysics and human potential. Learn about the newest books in spiritual guidance, natural healing, astrology, occult philosophy, and more. Enjoy book reviews, new age articles, a calendar of events, plus current advertised products and services. To get your free copy of *Llewellyn's New Worlds of Mind and Spirit,* send your name and address to:

Llewellyn's New Worlds of Mind and Spirit
P.O. Box 64383-K334, St. Paul, MN 55164-0383, U.S.A.